DEAR LITTLE, YOUR DOG SAYS HI! LOVE, GOD

A LOVE LETTER FROM HEAVEN'S PUPS TO THEIR FAVORITE EARTHLY HUMANS

WRITTEN & ILLUSTRATED BY D. LEE HILLS

A REBELLIOUS RAVEN PUBLISHING CO. & BOOK STORE PUBLICATION

Published by Rebellious Raven Pub Co. LLC
P.O. Box 249
Soddy-Daisy, TN 37384
www.rebelliousravenpubcollc.com

ISBN: 979-8-9895695-1-9
Library of Congress Control Number: 2025911374

This book is a work of fiction. Names, characters, places, and incidents are either the product of the author's imagination or are used fictitiously. Any resemblance to actual persons, living or dead, events, or locales is entirely coincidental.

Designed by Rebellious Raven Pub Co LLC
Printed in the USA
First Printing: June 2025

10 9 8 7 6 5 4 3 2 1

This book is dedicated to my mom
- Donna Marie Rabbett -
who began collecting stray and abandoned angels at the
earliest of ages, and brought that tradition into my
childhood.

She didn't warn me about the inexplicable heartache that
comes when it's time to give them back to God— and for
that I am also grateful. Had I known, I may never have
had the courage to discover how worth it it all is.

So thank you, Mom,
for introducing me to angels, for entertaining them,
for letting them both fill and break your heart,
and for passing your courage, your strength, and your
eternal well of love for these beings
(and their magic) on to me.

DEAR LITTLE,
I WRITE TO TELL YOU IN THIS
LETTER FROM ABOVE,
THAT THERE'S A SPECIAL SOMEONE
HERE WITH ME,
SENDING YOU A MESSAGE OF
COMFORT AND LOVE.

POSTCARD

YOUR FAITHFUL
KEEPER & FURRY
COMPANION, YOUR
SILLY 4-LEGGED FRIEND,
IS WATCHING OVER YOU
WITH GRATITUDE,
AND HOLDING YOUR HEART
WHILE IT MENDS.

NOW, BEFORE I GO ON, THERE'S SOMETHING ABOUT HEAVEN YOU SHOULD KNOW-- YOU MIGHT THINK AS YOU LOOK AT THE PICTURES I'VE SENT, THAT YOUR POOCH LOOKS A LITTLE DIFFERENT IN HEAVEN'S GLOW--

AND THERE MAY BE A FEW REASONS...

FOR EXAMPLE,
SOME WEAR WINGS OR HALOS NOW,
SOME CHOOSE DIFFERENT COLORS EVERY DAY.
ALSO, SOME OF THE PICTURES
MIGHT BE BLURRY
BECAUSE YOUR LOVING FRIEND
AND THEIR BUDDIES
WERE JUST TOO EXCITED TO SIT AND STAY.

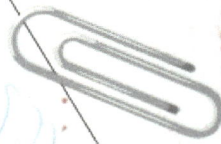

POSTCARD

This Space for Writing Messages

SO IF YOU THINK YOU
SEE YOUR FURBALL,
AND FEEL EXCITED AND
RELIEVED,
YOUR DOG PUT THAT
LOVE IN THE PICTURE,
SO, THAT YOU WOULD
KNOW IT IS YOUR
PUPPO INDEED!

Place
Stamp
Here

PostCard

THIS SPACE FOR WRITING MESSAGES

SOMETIMES WE CALL YOUR FRIEND "WAGSTER", "WAGMEISTER", AND "WAGGA-DOODLE-DOO" BECAUSE OF THE FULL-BODY-WAG THAT COMES

ANYTIME WE MENTION YOU, (WHICH WE OFTEN DO).

PLACE STAMP HERE

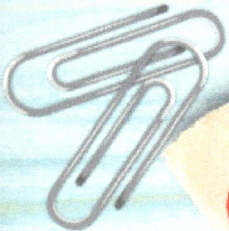

THERE IS NO PAIN
OR SORROW HERE IN HEAVEN,
ONLY PURE DELIGHT.
ALL DOGS HAVE THEIR FAVORITE TOYS,
FAVORITE FOODS, FAVORITE BLANKIES,
AND GET TO WATCH
THEIR FAVORITE MOVIES AT NIGHT.

YOUR PUP
GETS TO RUN AND PLAY,
AND TUSSLE
ON COTTON-CANDY CLOUDS.
SOMETIMES THE FUR BABY WILL
SIT OR ROLL OVER,
JUST TO KEEP MAKING YOU
PROUD.

In heaven's parks and on our slides,
with sprinklers, balls and swings...
All the dogs play, dig,
zoom and bop
on wagging tail springs.

FULL-BELLIED AND SLEEPY AFTER THE PLAYING ENDS.

THEY CATCH FRISBEES MID-AIR, AND THEY LOVE AND PROTECT THEIR FRIENDS. THEY DO TAPPSIES WITH THEIR TOE-BEANS DURING DINNER-

IN THIS
HEAVENLY REALM,
WHERE JOY
IS ALWAYS IN THE AIR,
THE PUPS CELEBRATE FREEDOM
FROM THINGS THEY FOUND UNFAIR.

Among the
fluffy clouds,
where their paws
are forever clean;
no more worries about
baths, vet visits, thunder
or stupid nail-trimmings.

In fluffy beds,
with soft pillows and
blankets galore,
all the doggos puppy
pile,
cuddle, snuggle,
and snore.

DID YOURS ALWAYS SNORE SO LOUD?

EVEN IN THEIR SLUMBER,
LITTLE PAWS TWITCH TO THEIR
FAVORITE BEATS.
PEACEFULLY DREAMING, KNOWING
THEY WILL WAKE TO THEIR FAVORITE
TOYS AND TREATS.

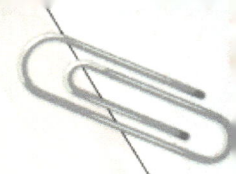

THE PUPS HERE OBVIOUSLY HAVE A DIFFERENT LANGUAGE THEY SPEAK, WITH BARKS AND WOOFS, EXPRESSIVE EYES, DROOL THEY FLING & LEAK···

BUT I'M GOD, SO I ALWAYS KNOW

OF FUN ADVENTURES, CUDDLES, AND MIRTH.

WHEN
THEY'RE TALKING
OF THEIR LOVE
FOR THEIR HUMANS BELOW.
THEY TELL STORIES
TO ONE ANOTHER
ABOUT THEIR TIME ON EARTH-
OF BEING SAVED,
OF MUDDY PAWS,

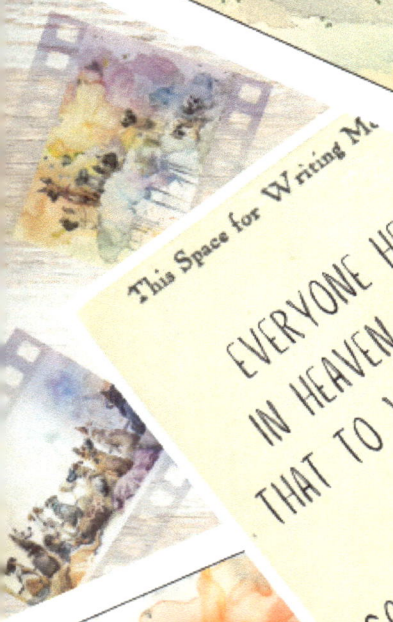

POST CARD

Place Stamp Here
Domestic One cent
Foreign Two cents

THAT WE ALL
WATCH YOU
FROM THE STARS ...

This Space for Writing M...

EVERYONE HERE
IN HEAVEN KNOWS
THAT TO YOU WE SEEM
SO FAR.

SO, YOUR DOG WANTED
ME TO TELL YOU, ALSO,

PostCard

BECAUSE EVEN AMIDST THE JOY, THE FREEDOM, AND THE PLAY, YOUR BABY STILL THINKS ABOUT YOU SEVERAL TIMES A DAY.

PLACE STAMP HERE

THEY KNOW YOU WANT TO TOUCH AND SNUGGLE THEM, FEEL THEM BY YOUR SIDE, AND YOUR PUPPY-DOG SEES THE TEARS

AS THEY GATHER IN YOUR EYES.

So, do you understand,
sweet little,
that amidst the silliness and eternal
play,
they love you so much
that when they know you are sad,
it can be difficult for them to stay?

SO THEY WHISPER TO ME
EACH TIME THEY SEE YOU CRY,
"PLEASE COMFORT MY HUMAN,
AND LET THEM KNOW I AM NEARBY."

WELL, SWEET LITTLE, THAT'S
PRETTY MUCH YOUR PUP'S NOTE,
AND THIS LETTER IS LONGER
THAN I THOUGHT IT WOULD BE,

BUT I'VE INCLUDED A FEW MORE PICTURES OF HEAVEN, SO THAT YOU CAN SEE MORE OF WHAT YOUR PUP SEES.

POST CARD

Place Stamp Here
Domestic
One cent
Foreign
Two cents

This Space for Writing M...

"DO I KNOW THEM
EACH PERSONALLY?"
YOU ASK...
OF COURSE, THEY
ARE THE BEST THING
I'VE EVER MADE!

THAT'S WHY I CALL THEM BACK
TO ME SO QUICKLY,
AND THEN SEND MORE IN TRADE.

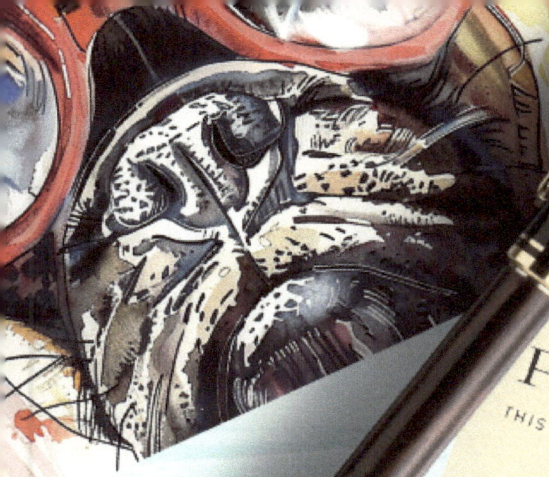

POSTCARD
THIS SPACE FOR WRITING MESSAGES

OK, NOW, WHAT IS YOUR
POOCH'S NAME?
_____
(ANGEL'S NAME HERE)

AH, YES, WE
KNOW EACH
OTHER WELL!

I HAVE TO THANK YOU
FOR SHARING YOUR DOGGO WITH
US HERE.
YOURS HAS BEEN THE GOODEST!
THOUGH, I AM NOT SUPPOSED
TO TELL....

SO, SWEET LITTLE,
JUST REMEMBER THAT YOUR
FURRY FRIEND LOVES YOU
EVEN MORE AS TIME
PASSES BY

AND IN SHORT WE'VE
WRITTEN THIS LETTER
TO TELL YOU, YOUR DOG
SAYS, "HI"!

PLACE
STAMP
HERE

S.54

AJ Abby Abraham Ace Adler Aiden Aika Albert Alfie Amanda Angel Annie Apollo April Archie Ariel Arthur Ashley Asia Aspen Athena Atlas Ava Babba Baby Bacon Baila Bailey Ballerina Balta Balou Bam Bambi Bandit Banksy Barkley Barney Barron Basil Baxter Baylee Bean Bear Beau Bella Belle Ben Benito Benny Bentley Benton Beretta Bernie Betsy Betty Bikki Bimmer Bingo Bino Birdy Biscuit Bishop Bitboy Bitsie Bjorn Bjuki Blackjack Blanca Blaze Blenheim Blixma Blu-Blah Blue Bo Bob Bobo Bonzi Boo Boomer Boon Bosley Boss Boxer Bozo Brady Brand y Brindi Bristol Brita Britton Brodi Bronson Brood Brownie Bruce Bruno Brutus Bubba Buck Bud Buddha Buddy Buffy Bugs Bui Bullseye Bunny Buster Butters Cadillac Caine Cali Callie Calypsa Cami Cara Cash Casper Cass Cassidy Cece Cersei Chablis Champy Chance Chandler Chaplain Charli Charlie Charlotte Cheeky Cheesebob Cheetah Chester Chetti Chewbacca Chewy Chex Chibi Chico Chili Chingon Chip Chloe Choco Choi Chooch Chopper Chu-Chu Chuggie Cinder Cippy Clippy Cleo Clove Clover Clyde Cobi Coco Cocoa Cody Conan Cookie Cooper Cricket Crunch Cuddles Cupcake Dae-z Daisy Dakota Dali Dallas Damien Darwin Dash Davi David DaVinci Dax Deezy Deja Delilah Dengal Denver Deogee Dexter Diamond Diesel Dino Disco Diva Dixie Dizzle DJ Dobby Doc Dodge Domino Doodlebug Dolly Donnie Dory Dottie Dover Dozer Ducky Dudley Duke Dulci Dundee Dunkin Dusty Echo Eddie Eggsy Eleanor Ella Ellie Elsie Elvie Elvira Emily Emma Emmett Enzo Esme Esteban Eugene Evee Ezra Faye Feisty Felix Fendi Fenway Fergus Fido Filbert Finley Finn Finnick Fiona Fletcher Flossie Floyd Fluffy Fotis Foxy Fozzy Frankie Freckles Fred Fresh Fudge Gabby Gadget Gander Gator Gatsby George Gibbs Gidget Gigi Gilly Gilmore Ginger Giovanni Girl Gizmo Goldie Goose Gotti Grace Gracie Graussie Gregory Greta Gretchen Grimmie Groot Gucci Guera Guiness Gunner Gus-Gus Gypsy Ham Hank Hannah Hans Hardy Harley Harlow Harper Harry Haven Hayva Hazel Hector Heidi Henry Hera Hercules Hermoine Henry Hershey Hippy Holden Hogan Hollie Holly Honey Honey-bun Hoss Houdini Howard Hugs Humpty Indiana Indy Ingrid Inky Jac Jack Jackson Jake Jane Jarvis Jasper Jax Jazz Jedi Jeep Jenga Jessie Jethro Jett Jiggy Jimmy Jingle-bell Jinx Jojo Joplin Jordan Jordy Josie Jovie Joy-Joy Juice Juno Justice Kahlua Kai Kaiser Kal Kane Kalo Karmella Katrina Kato Kawaii Keeley Keiko Keizhy Kilmer Keeper Kermit Kevin Khloe Kiah Kiki Kiko

Killa Kilo Kitten Knox Koa Koda Kozmo Koa Koda Kozmo Krystal Kujo Lacee Lady Ladybug Laila Lakota Lani Laurie Lava Layla Leddy Leelou Lennon Leo León Leroy Levi Lexi Liam Liesel Lightening Lil-Bit Lily Lil Man Lincoln Lindsay Linus Loki Lola Lollipop Louby Louie Luca Lucky Lucy Lula Luna Mabel Mable Mackey Maddie Maddux Madison Maggie Magic Magoo Magnus Maisie Major Malibu Manny Manolo ManU Marble Marie Marigold Marley Marlo Marlow Marple Marshal Martini Mary Matilda Mattie Maude Maui Maverick Max Maximus Maycee Maya McGregor Meeko Mercy Merlin Mia Millie Milo Mira Miso Missy Misty MJ Modoe Moe Mojo Momma Mona Monkey Monte Monty Moo Morgan Mr. Bean Mr. Puddles Mr. Rogers Muckers Mugsy Mushu MyTy Nala Nanuk Neeko Neeny Neil Nelli Nelly Neo Nero NewGirl Nia Nikki Nilla Nimbus Nina Niya Noel Nola Nova Nugget Nunzo Oakley Oatmeal Odie Olive Oliver Ollie Oreo Orion Oscar Otto Ozzie Opie Paisley Panda Papa Patches Patrick Patsy Peaches Peanut Pearl Penelope Pebbles Penny Pepper Peter Petey Petunia Phoebe Phil Piglet Pinch Pinky Piper Pippa Pippin Pixie Pizza-Roll PJ Pluto Poco Pogi Pokey Pooh Poppy Potter Presley Prince Princess Puddles Pudgy Puff Puppas Quincey Radar Raffi Raiden Raisin Ralphie Rambo Rami Randy-Pandy Rascal Raven Red Remmie Remmy Rex Ricochet Ricki Ricky Riley Ringo Ripley Riss Rocco Rocky Roger Rolo Roman Ron a Roo-Roo Roscoe Rose Rosebud Rosemary Rosie Roxanne Roxette Roxy Rozlyn Ruby Rufus Ruger Rumi Ruxin Rusty Ryder Sable Sadie Sailor Saint Sally Sambo Sammy Sampson Sarge Sasha Sassy Sausage Sawyer Scarlett Schatzi Scooby Scout Scratch Scrappy Sephy Sensi Shadow Shae Shakis Shiko Shelby Shooter Sigman Siku Simba Singer Sinjin Skye Slate Slam Smokey Snort Snow Snowy Snickers Snoopy Snuggles Soldier Sonny Sophie Sosa Spade Sparky Slam Sparrow Splash Sprocket Stella Stink Stitch Sterling Story Sugar Sully Sunny Sweaters Sydney Taffy Takillya Tank Tara Tasha Tater Taz Teddy Tezla Theo Thor Thumper Thunder Tiara Tickle Tiger Tigger Tillie Tilly Timber Tiny Tin-Tin Tissy Titan Toby Tofu Tommy Tootie Tootsie Tooty-Bug Travis Trigger Trimmy Tripp Trixie Tucker Tuffy Tulip Tully Turvey Twinkie Twix Tyson Unsoo Uriel Vader Veera Victor Vino Violet Voodoo Waffles Wallace Whiskey Wicket Wiley Willow Wilson Winnie Winston Winter Wolfie Wonder Wyatt Xanadu Xander Xena Xeno Yoda Yogi Yuki Zachary Zane Zara Zeke Zelda Zena Zephyr Zeus Ziggyv Ziva Zoe Zoey Zorro

www.ingramcontent.com/pod-product-compliance
Lightning Source LLC
Chambersburg PA
CBHW060829270326
41931CB00003B/112